MARY DORCEY

The River That Carries Me

SALMON POETRY

For Monica

I wish to thank Gráinne Healy, agent extraordinaire, Susan Forsythe and Valclusa, Greg Cahill for being there and Máire Dorcey for the start of it all.

Published in 1995 by
Salmon Publishing Ltd,
Upper Fairhill, Galway

© Mary Dorcey 1995

The moral right of the author has been asserted.

The Publishers gratefully acknowledge the support of The Arts Council.

A catalogue record for this book is available from the British Library.

ISBN 1 897648 62 6

Cover photography by Fergus Bourke
Cover design by Poolbeg Group Services Ltd
Set by Poolbeg Group Services Ltd in Goudy
Printed by Colour Books, Baldoyle Ind Est, Dublin 13.

Contents

The Breath of History

I am not an ordinary woman.
I wake in the morning.
I have food to eat.
No one has come in the night
to steal my child, my lover.
I am not an ordinary woman.

A plum tree
blossoms outside my window,
the roses are heavy with dew.
A blackbird sits on a branch
and sings out her heart.
I am not an ordinary woman.

I live where I want.
I sleep when I'm tired.
I write the words I think.
I can watch the sky
and hear the sea.
I am not an ordinary woman.
No one has offered me life
in exchange for another's.

No one has beaten me until I fall down.
No one has burnt my skin
nor poisoned my lungs.
I am not an ordinary woman.
I know where my friends live.
I have books to read,

I was taught to read.
I have clean water to drink.
I know where my lover sleeps;
she lies beside me,
I hear her breathing.
My life is not commonplace.

At night the air
is as sweet as honeysuckle
that grows along the river bank.
The curlew cries
from the marshes
far out,

high and plaintive.
I am no ordinary woman.
Everything I touch and see
is astonishing and rare –
privileged.
Come celebrate each
privileged, exceptional thing:
water, food, sleep –
the absence of pain –
a night without fear –
a morning without
the return of the torturer.

A child safe,
a mother,
a lover, a sister.
Chosen work.
Our lives are not commonplace –
any of us who read this.

But who knows –
tomorrow or the day after . . .
I feel all about me
the breath of history –
pitiless
and ordinary.

I Cannot Love You as You Want to be Loved

I cannot love you
as you want to be loved –
without wanting.
I cannot love you
without loving your black startled eyes –
without wanting them to look at me.
Without wanting to see them
catch fire
as they look at me.

I cannot love you
without loving your thighs –
the long lovely line of your thighs.
Without wanting to run my hand along the length of them.
I cannot love you
without loving your hands –
so strong, so talkative.
Without wanting them to touch me,
to touch my hand,
my thigh.
I cannot love you as you want to be loved –
without wanting.

You are a blade
I have lifted from my own hand
to put a stop to wounding.
Who made you so sharp?
so dangerous?

I miss your laughter
and your flights of fancy.
Your foolishness,
your wild untamable ways.
I miss your passion for things –
your refusal to take life quietly.

You are a blade
I have lifted from my own hand
to put a stop to wounding.
Who made you so sharp?
so dangerous?
You whose love words
were like a bounty;
a burst of grace,
oiled and perfumed –
each one a healing,
a benediction.
You whose eyes were pools
stars could bathe in.

You are a knife
I have lifted from my own hand
to put a stop to wounding.
You should be the earth I lie down upon,
the river that carries me,
the bright sky that covers me,
the wind that sings through the lilac.
Who made you a blade
I cannot dare to handle?

You Will Not Turn

You will not turn.
You will not turn.
I have seen for the last time,
the last smile
on your mouth,
the last curse.

I have seen for the last time
the last look,
the last touch of fingers to lips;
the last kiss blown out.
You will not turn.

I have heard the last word of anger,
the last of love.
I have felt the last caress,
the last glance of your skin
against mine.

An end to weeping,
An end to laughter.
An end to last times
of weeping
of laughter.
You will not turn again.

We have said goodbye
without saying it.
We have said no words:
no words of hope,
of regret.

No words at last.
Not even goodbye.
No turning back.
The last smile,
the last tear.
And if in the last moment

you should raise your arm
and give the last wave of your hand;
the last sign,
I will not see,
because I am walking away from you
love,
and will not turn.
Will not turn.

Learning to Live With It

They took my pulse
and my temperature.
They told me to lie down
and be sensible.

They said all things,
bad and good come to an end.
Half a lifetime of love –
let it be enough for you.

They said I must study the alphabet –
and learn to read the writing on the wall.
They said I must come to face facts –
they handed me the blindfold.

They said I must stop listening
for the last cry from the wilderness.
They said I must stop asking –
they showed me how to cut out my tongue.

And you? Well, you, they said,
always made too much of things.
They saw the blood slipping from your eyes –
they offered you their handkerchief.

When the flesh withered on your frame
and your cheeks grew haggard
They said: See – how shapely she is –
what fine bones!

They told me to lie down and be sensible.
They said all things come to an end.
I must stop listening, they said,
for the last cry from the wilderness.

I must stop searching through grains of sand
for one grain of sand.
I must stop holding out bare arms
to stem the tide.

And when you cried out in your sleep –
Love me still love, my only love
They said: See –
she's learning to live with it!

The Making of Poetry

I will have to stop this,
I told myself
– this making of phrases;
this word spinning,
if all that inspires it
is grief.

And not that
I wasn't joyous,
often –
even careless
in that time.
But writing will not be shaped
from the surface happiness of mood.

Pleasure
like sorrow
must seep
down
to lodge in the marrow,
before
filtered,
it rejoins the bloodstream
and courses back
to feed the heart
and poetry.

Stone Deaf

All along the sand –
a stone's throw
from the sea,
the stones lie scattered.
The sea sighs and sucks.
The stones shine and shiver
but the sea
doesn't see.
And the stones
are stone deaf.

Teach Me to Remember

Teach me to remember
a Spanish town –
white cups, strong coffee,
shutters drawn in late afternoon
against the flight of swallows.
Teach me to remember
a house overlooking western seas;
the shifting light
on stone and pasture.

Music on high starred
winter nights;
opening the door
to find sheep lured
from the mountains
to listen.
Picking wild flowers in summer:
flag iris, bog cotton
carried home by the armful.

Talking politics
at breakfast,
shopping for dinner
in small country towns;
driving home through dark streets
in silence
rain falling
your hand on my knee.

You want me to learn
not to want
but I'm not good at it.
I don't know how
to half want
or half forget.

Can you teach me how to remember
a beach at evening,
the gorse in full bloom
the sky livid;
we two walking
and not remember your arm
slipping through mine –
the exact touch of your skin
at the elbow
as it slides against mine?
Snow on a roof under moonlight,
a poppy growing wild at the roadside.
The way your breath catches
with joy,
with surprise.

Teach me to remember
a village in Greece,
the sheep belling their passage
through the fields,
and you,
without a word of the language
making a friend of
every old woman
and child in the streets.

You who are moderate in nothing;
who never knew what a line was –
much less where to draw it,
will you teach me?
Someone must.

Teach me to remember
without wanting it back.

It Began With my Hands

It began with my hands –
your death.
My hands that would not
touch yours again.
The joints of my fingers
grew stiff.
My palms ached.

Your hands
that I loved –
strong, graceful, curious.
You thought with them
and lived by them.
I remember how they touched
everything you saw.
Your death took place first
in my hands.
After that

it was time for my sight –
your dark wild eyes
dying in mine.
I could look at nothing.
Every colour hurt,
every shape.
Even dusk startled me.
In the morning,
on waking,
no need to open them.

Where would I look
if not into your eyes?
Not much later
it reached my voice.
My throat grew hoarse.
Your voice
that I would not hear again;
that sings when you speak,
was fading in mine
note by note.

Until at last no sound at all
would come from my tongue.
But what need had I of speech
if you would not hear?
And your hair –

Did I say that my own turned gray?
The dark wool of your hair
that would not spring
at my touch again
was dying in mine.
I could feel the roots
wither
strand by strand.
I am not exaggerating
this is how
it was.

Your death
is taking place in my flesh
hour by hour,
cell by cell.
What will be left me
at the end of it?
Any element
proof against it?
One shred
resistant
from which new life
can be grafted?

Memory.

Trees

The trees stand
on the side of the mountain,
in the rain.
Not doing anything,
just waiting.
Or do I only imagine
they are waiting –
and for what?
Yes, I imagine them
waiting
because it isn't possible
to imagine them
standing there,
all these centuries –
and not waiting,
for something.

The Good Times

And still this dream of you:
the dream of the good times,
the good times to come.
My life with you almost over
and still this dream of the good times,
the good times to come.

It seems
we were just getting started.
Have I been waiting half my life
for my life with you to begin,
for the good times
to come?

And still the dream
of the curtain rising
and there on the stage
waiting,
the perfect day –
the good times to come.
But that day was always tomorrow,

and tomorrow came suddenly –
slipped into yesterday.
And took with it,
for safekeeping –
the good times.

I Have Your Name

I have your name
and no use for it.
It will never call you home again.

I have all your names still:
everyone of them,
on the tip of my tongue.
I have to bite my lip
to keep from spilling them.
Useless now –
nobody comes.
I have your name and no use for it.

I have said it
times without number,
without thinking,
not needing to think.
I have called it though the years,
winter and summer,
early and late.
First thing in the morning,
and last at night;

like a child
from sleep
certain of your coming.
I have called it like a mother
when no other sound would do,
when there were no words and no gestures,
only your name
said against cold, against fright.

I have called it across empty rooms
and crowded ones
and waited for your head to turn.
I loved waiting for your head to turn.
I have your name and no use for it.
I have spoken it on land
and sea.
Across three continents.

I have said it in rapture,
in anger,
in grief.
I have called it across fields;
bellowed into the wind,
like a farmer calling home the dogs
and had it blown back on my lips.
I have murmured it so softly
no one heard but you.

I have your name and no use for it.
No matter where
I say it now:
how loudly
or how often –
it will never
call you home.

Tell Me How You Carry it Off

Tell me how to do it.
You must know how
because you've chosen it,
or say you have.

I don't know –
I can't imagine.
But you must, surely
because you've chosen.

So tell me how
you carry it off –
it must be easy
if you've done it.

Teach me –
if it's the last thing you
teach me,
how you manage it –
how you live without me.

So that I can learn –
how to live
without
you.

The Last Word

And all my sorrow
lies in this –
I chose to go
but not the manner of my going.
I walked away from years of loving,
thinking I could take
the best of it
on my back,
stored with clothes and books
in a haversack.

But you had other ideas –
(I might have known)
You locked the stable door
as soon as I had bolted.
If you could not
keep me in –
you would keep me out.

When I tried to remonstrate
you took up silence.
And so
you who always had
the last word –
by refusing all speech –
have it still.

And I?
What have I kept?
Some letters and photographs
in a haversack.
And slipped between their folds,
unnoticed
until now,
all the regrets
you have sent packing.

This Day I have Turned my Back on Sorrow

Enough of this.
I have had enough of repining,
of loss and lament.

Enough.
I want to dance in the street.
I want laughter –
loud days and wild nights.
I will make it up,
if I have to
until it happens.
I will make it happen
if I have to.

I have had enough of repenting,
of loss
and lament.
I want
dancing in the streets,
laughter.

I will go into the fields
and under a white hawthorn tree
dig a grave
six foot deep.
Into it I will put
regret and remorse.
I will cover it up,
shovel the clay
and lay down my cross.

I have had enough
of lament
and loss.
After all
I wrote my own story,
chose my course.
I brought myself
to this edge of this river.

Enough.
It is over;
the sad times
the bleak.
Put behind me.
I have taken what I need –
the few things of value
salvaged from the wreck.
I carry them in my flesh and blood
until the last day.

Enough of loss and lament.
I want to dance in the street
I want laughter
luminous mornings, long nights.
It is over
finished,
remorse and lament

I have buried them,
turned the clay
six foot deep, under
the white hawthorn tree.

This day
I have turned my back
on sorrow.

Walking on Air

She stood before me,
she stretched her cloak
over the chasm that lay between our lives.

See she said –
it's a bridge – trust me!
Cross over.

And I stepped over
the abyss that lay between our lives.
I walked across the bridge

she made with her cloak
as if walking on air.
When I reached the other side

I looked back.
I saw no bridge.
Only a great chasm stretching behind me.

Look, I said,
there was no bridge.
I might have plunged to my death.

I might have died.
But she stood regarding me,
her cloak wrapped tight about her.

Well, it doesn't matter
she said,
you're here aren't you?

You got to the other side?
Trembling I moved on
past her.

A little further along the way
another woman stood
by the side of a river.

Smiling
she held out her hand.
Don't be afraid, she said,

let me help you.
She stretched out her arm over
the dark water that flowed between us.

See, she said,
it's a bridge – cross over!
Trust me.

I see no bridge, I said,
only your arms
stretched wide.

Yes, she said,
I have stretched my arms
over the torrent

between us – trust me!
I am a bridge
I will bear your weight

long enough.
I looked at the chasm
that yawned between our lives

and the raging torrent.
How long is enough, I asked.
As long as it takes,

she said.
So I closed my eyes
and stepped into her bare arms.

Crocus

You would want me
to tell you, I think –
even at the cost
of long distance –
that the crocuses
we planted last fall
have bloomed.

A Leather Jacket

I remember the creaking of leather –
the sleeves of a leather jacket
creaking
as my arms tighten about you.

The leather
plaintive, supplicant.
A sound I had never noticed before,
a steady, soft moan.

Sharp and soft
like the crack of an oar
turning in its spur.
Wood in steel

creaking as it turns slowly
back and forth.
And the sound the water
makes as it slips swiftly

along its length.
Glistening as far as the blade
to fall
drop by smooth drop.

Breaking the polished surface,
to spread it wide
in slowly widening circles
that travel outwards

and beyond.
And the blade of the oar
comes after, striking down
to cut the water

sheer, and sinking
is engulfed –
bent to the shape
of water.

And struggling,
lifts clear
up into the light
and draws again

across the glittering
surface,
a diamond track of
water.

I miss the sound of leather –
a leather jacket;
its sleeves creaking softly
as my arms tighten about you.

Night Passage

Night passage is the best thing
neither leaving nor arriving.
A ship travelling in darkness
between here and there.

I thought it was the city
I wanted.
I went to the city.
But it was too much for me.
Too many talking,
too many breathing,
too many watching
so as not to be seen watching.

I went to the country.
thinking I wanted the quiet,
the space of it, the open skies.
But at night
the silence woke up
and stalked me about the house.
It knocked against the furniture
and rattled the air
until my heart rang like a bell.

There have been places crowded by you
and places desolate for the want of you.
Sooner or later
everywhere becomes somewhere.
Night passage is the best thing
before there becomes here.

The First Morning

There will never be another morning
like the first morning.
And there will never be another face
like yours –
waking to the first morning.

Like Joy in Season

So already,
your hair is falling;
snapping loose from the comb
like leaves in autumn.
Bright and gold;
falling
strand by strand.

No matter
who needs it?
You can camp it up –
take to hats;
audacious, unsuitable.
Or stride like a rockstar
bald headed.

And for eyebrows,
how will you manage?
Paint them on high and garish?
Or leave them bare,
so that
you may delight in the air
of taking all this
without the least show
of surprise?

And the experts say,
that you will not
necessarily,
lose
teeth or nails.
Now isn't that something
to be going on with!
In this tooth and nail combat
you find yourself waging.

And if you are sometimes sick
and sometimes tired,
which of us isn't –
either or both
sometimes or often?

And you who are so often
glad and laughing,
can spare a little tiredness.
And pain passes
at last,
like joy.

Like joy
which catches us out,
startling the heart even in these –
or especially these
surprising times.

And if it is only
at night
when you have stopped
laughing
or talking,
or loving.

If it is only at night
that your hair
is heard falling:
bright blonde hair
snapping from the roots
like twigs from a branch –

like leaves falling.
Well, leaves grow back in season.
Like joy in season –
like sorrow.

Two Mothers

She spreads the paper.
Her son writes from Africa:
the fields of dust,
the bones of camel and cattle
littering the desert.
The desert reaching its grip
right to the walls of the town.

She lifts her coffee cup.
Imagine all the strange sights
he is seeing today, she says,
while we sit here reading.

She smiles at the photograph of her son,
hungry for news of him;
proud that someone has thought
it worth paying
to send him all that way
to a place she cannot imagine,
though she tries.

He writes
that the woman standing
outside the mud hut
offered to pay the man
who took her photograph.
She has her pride
and cameras and newsprint
have magic
on both sides of the equator.

Two women alone.
One in Africa.
One in Ireland.
Both widows.
One has lost her children
to emigration:
to foreign countries
she will never see
where the money is better.

The other has lost
her children to famine.
Has watched them die
at her side.
The children
who had no money
to leave for other places.

Both women have learned
to pay attention to the journalist.
One, because the newspaper
brings word of her son
who is far away;
perhaps in danger
in a place she cannot imagine.

The other
because after the camera
and the strange questions
will come sacks of grain,
sent by people in places
she cannot imagine.

The woman with the newspaper reads on.
She is no longer smiling.
She imagines
the camel dying in the dry fields,
the desert reaching
to the walls of the town
the crying of children;

She imagines a mother
watching a child starve –
a daughter or a son.
She imagines a journalist
who earns a living
taking pictures
of the dying.

A Woman in Another War

Somedays when we kiss
we close our eyes.
Somedays when we close our eyes
we kiss.
Somedays we do not read the newspaper.

A woman was getting on a bus,
I was reading the newspaper.
The woman carried a baby in a carry cot –
Mind your step, another woman said,
and offered her a seat.

I was reading the newspaper –
I was reading the story
of a woman in another country,
a woman in another war.
The story of a woman
who was raped by soldiers.

The soldiers came into her town.
They ordered the women into the street,
they told them to lie on the ground.
They made them lie in rows
and the soldiers raped them
in rows.
One woman after another.
One soldier after another.

One of the women
had a baby,
a newborn baby.
It lay on the earth beside her.
It cried to be fed.
She heard it cry.
She asked the man who was raping her
to stop – to stop
long enough to let her
feed her child.

Bring me my child, she said.
The man stopped.
He got up from her body
and lifted the baby.
He carried it in his arms,
he held it over her.
He took out a knife,
he smiled.
He cut the child's neck from its shoulders
and held the bleeding head
to the woman's breast:
Here's your baby, he said,
feed it.

There was a woman in another country,
a woman in another war.
The soldiers came into the town,
they ordered the women into the streets.
They raped them one after another,
row after row;
one soldier after another,
one woman after another.

The woman on the bus
was helped by another
to sit down.
She lifted the baby
from its cot.
You have to be careful of the head,
the other woman said.
Yes, the woman answered
and with her hand
she cradled the baby's head.

Somedays when we kiss
we close our eyes.
Somedays when we close our eyes
we kiss.
Somedays we don't read the newspaper.

Reading the Newspaper

Where were we on that day?
Were we somewhere else?
Yes, we were somewhere else...

That day we were somewhere else.
And what were we doing?
Were we reading a book,

Or making tea?
Or were we giving birth
Or having a dance?

Yes I think that day we were reading a book.
Or were we buying shoes?
Or making dinner?

Or going to a funeral,
Or having a drink?
Yes I think that day we were buying shoes.

Or were we paying our tv licence?
Or our car tax was it?
Or the insurance was it?

Yes I think that day we were paying our tv licence.
Or were we coming home from the office?
Or doing the shopping?

Or having our hair done?
Yes, I think that day we were having our hair done.
Or were we making money?

Was that it?
Or something special for lunch?
Or making a speech?

Or making love? Yes, I think
That day we were having a love affair.
I remember your mouth kissing my eyes.

Kissing them shut.
Yes, I think that day we were making love.
Or writing a poem.

Were we writing a poem?
Yes I think that day
I was writing a poem.

I think I remember writing it.
It might even have been this poem.
Yes, I think that day I was writing this poem

About a woman who was raped
That day,
In some other country.

Some other war.
And when her baby cried
They cut off its head.

Yes I think that day
We were making tea.
I think that day we were making love.

I think that day we were giving birth.
I think that day
We were reading the newspaper.

On Looking at a Photograph of Women Entitled: 'Standing in Line.'

Tall or short,
cropped hair;
blonde or dark,
the women stand in line.
Balancing a baby on their hip,
holding an older child by the hand.
They stand so still,
so patiently;
keeping the children quiet.
They look so womanly,
so ordinary.

They might be women anywhere.
Waiting for anything.
Women do so much waiting:
for the bus,
or the opening of a shop,
for food rations,
or at the school gate,
or the doctor's surgery.

Except for the curious fact of their being naked,
these women.
I see their white limbs,
the wide hips,
clutching a child with one arm,
the other reaching down to grasp an uplifted hand.
They are staring ahead,

their hollow eyes
expressionless.
Why are they naked?
Their flesh so fragile,
so exposed?
Their eyes so blank?

What are they waiting for?
For a swimming pool?
The beach?
For public showers?
Yes, that's it –
when I look closely
the caption reads:
'Women standing in line
waiting for the showers.'

Now looking again
I see how thin they are:
the high shoulders –
the hips blade-like.
Their children lean against them,
faces hidden from the camera,
the way tired children anywhere
lean into a mother's side,
after a long day out.

I imagine them asking
the questions children always ask.
And their mothers answering
as mothers always do:
No – I don't know what we're waiting for.
Yes – I'm tired too.
Yes – we'll be going home soon.
I promise.

The children pressed close
to their mothers
partly obscure their outline
which is why
I didn't notice immediately
how gaunt they are,
these women,
how tired,
how naked,
how quiet.

These women waiting
holding their children by the hand,
waiting for the showers to open.
Quieting their babies.
Waiting –
women do so much waiting.
Standing patiently in line.
It's the everydayness –
the quietness
that hurts.

A Bridge of People

Talkative with an old lover
or drunk alone in the small hours;
she has acknowledged more than once
that it was you – your image she sought
in every woman she drew close.
One had your dark hair and laughter,
another your roundabout way
of telling a story.
Yet another, your trick of taking time
with each small thing.
And the last – was it just the fine bone
of her shoulder?
It seems she has spent years
plaiting your life through hers,
from every sought after touch
or chance word.

But at other times
(nearer the surface or deeper?)
in dream or the first stifled
second of waking,
she has remembered the casual enmity,
the long years of conflict
when hate was the unspoken,
every day thing
between mother and daughter.
And at such times
(more frequent this side of thirty?)
it seems she has spent these rare

careless years, building
from hand picked circumstance,
a bridge of people and places
broad enough to come between you.

Small Distinctions

At first, I told myself
I loved you for your virtues:
your strength, your pride
your mouth's quick grace,
the secrets that your eyes create.
When I came to know
your vanity,
the easy malice of your tongue,
the cunning of your frailties,
I grew to hate
or said I loved inspite of.

But that was in our infancy.
Time has spun me round
and dazed the sense
of all such nice distinctions
as liking and dislike.
And now when you lift your hand
and twist it through your hair
or stroke your cheek,
is it that I love you still
or simply that your gestures
speak my mother tongue?

The Train

As the train pulled out
from the station
I remembered your hands
drawing back from mine.
Must I find you
in such incongruous places?
Must there always be
so many partings?

Nothing About You I Would Not Love

Ah, how I let myself go
in my love for you.
What wild extravagance of giving
I lavished on my ardour for you.
Nothing about you I could not,
would not love –
your small white breasts,
quick hands, black spite.
Your eyes round in wonder
or narrow with knowing.
Your tongue's soft caress,

its whip and sting.
The innocence of your success,
the craft of your failings.
Oh, what a time I had
letting myself be swept along
on the broad back
of your tortured soul, in the
yellow cat glow of your eyes.
But now I know better and have
my pride and other refinements
of wisdom and age.

Come Wild, Come Sweetly

Come wild – come sweetly.
Come with a flower after anger;
some frail blue blossom
offered for pardon.

Come proud – come shyly
Come with eyes brilliant
as flares on dark water
or still as a child's in sleep.

Come sad – come gaily.
Come without words
to give voice to silence
or with laughter to cajole
the most solemn displeasure.

Come quickly – come slowly.
Come with strong coffee
to console a bleak morning
or with wine
to waylay the dusk.

Come hesitant – come reckless
Come with a smile empty handed
or laden with plunder
bright rags from the streets.

Come late – come early
Come when I've waited in doubt all night
or before I've found
even the words to ask.

Come then come soon come now.
Come under come over come with me.

Come as if to stay forever.
And then as you leave me –
begin to come back.

Time to Kill

Sirens blaring
on the motor way –
I saw an ambulance
today –
passing out a hearse.
The ambulance was in a hurry,
fighting death at every minute.
Whereas the hearse –
had time to kill.

Miss Me a Little

Miss me, you said,
But only a little.

And I do.
But everywhere.

Every inch of me
Misses you a little.

And when I see you again
Your lips can travel

My whole body,
From the nape of my neck

To the soles of my feet,
Seeking one place

That missed you
More than another,

And you will not find it.
I miss you,

Every inch of me;
The length and breath

Of my flesh,
Misses you a little.

Folding a Sheet

You are the one person
I could tell
but I have never told.
You are the one
there would be satisfaction in telling
because you are the only one
who would care as much.

We look into each other's eyes
and smile.
You are washing the dishes,
probably
and I am drying them,
stacking them neatly
into your remembered places.

Or folding a sheet;
pulling back,
holding taut,
then letting go
and standing close.

We are having one of our talks,
when we talk of everything;
your past and mine,
happiness and sorrow.
When we talk of everything
except the one thing
I want to tell you tonight.

That I cannot tell you
because you are the only person
who would care enough.

You are smiling,
appealing for reassurance,
confirmation.
Did you get it right?
Could you have done better?
The only thing you wanted
was for us to be happy.

And I am protecting you
(why am I always protecting you?)
Telling you
that there is no sure course,
no right way
to be a mother.

But tonight I want to look into your face
and let you see it.
I want to tell you
the one thing you wanted
was too much to ask.
The one impossible demand.
I want to let go,
to let it out
the pain held fast in my heart.

I want to fill
the neat kitchen,
lay it on the table.
I want to say
look –
look at all the pain
of any life.
The life you dragged me into
conceiving me heedlessly,
letting me loose on all this
to be happy.

I want to show you
the suffering,
the failure
time and again
to be the only thing
you wanted –
happy.
I won't, of course
because you would blame yourself
or care as much.

But you are glad you were born?
you ask.
And I say yes,
I am, what else
can you tell a mother?

The Sweet, Eternal Now

Why do we measure happiness
by the pain of its absence
and hesitate to claim it
until it's lost?

What is it about joy
that makes us circumspect
when we find it so easy
to share grief?

We boast of it almost –
suffering.
Confide it to our friends,
compare

the worst times,
the greatest injury –
revel in it.
Nothing is too hard,

too terrible to bare
when it comes to grief.
But happiness
makes us modest.

We keep it to ourselves.
Cosset it, conceal it
as if
fearful of wounding

by exposure.
Or of rousing envy.
Afraid of tempting providence.
Afraid of looking spoilt.

We speak of it only
when it's over,
lost.
We see it then

for what it was –
acknowledge the depth of passion,
the particular moments of bliss.
Friends commiserate,

shake their heads
I never knew they say –
I never knew
how much it meant.

When I was wretched,
steeped in grief.
When every day hurt,
when I could talk

of little else.
And it seemed a lifetime
might be spent
retelling the one story;

I promised myself
that if happiness ever
found me out again,
I would claim it

while it filled my heart,
confide it while it shone.
While it brimmed in the eye
praise its beauty,

delight in its youth.
Celebrate the then and there.
So let me say it now
when the time is ripe –

Whisper it if necessary
so as not to offend.
Though I would like
to brag a little –

flaunt it, strut.
I will whisper –
so as not to tempt the fates
who might snatch it back

if they knew.
Let me say it now
while it's true –
that most rare,

unexpected
and every day grace
has found me.
This is all I have to dream

and all I have to give.
This is passion,
faith,
pleasure without end.

This is as high as it goes –
as deep.
This is ecstasy –
no less.

Joy.
And more than that.
This is hope,
lust,

life after death.
This is my heaven
and my daily bread.
I am risen

phoenix like
from the ashes of despair.
Made again
in her image.

Reinvented,
rebirthed
a woman in love.
That ordinary thing –

a woman
worthy of love.
Bathed in the sweet smell
of excess.

Anointed and blessed.
This is my miracle,
my commonplace –
my never to be again,

every day grace.
Let me say it now
while it's here,
while the word is made flesh;

let me brag –
let me flaunt it –
and if the fates are watching
let me wave my hand.

This is all I have to want
and all I have to give.
This is risk,
this is passion

and pleasure without end.
This is joy,
this is rapture.
This is not before

nor after.
This is the sweet,
eternal,
now.

When the Wind Blows Every Leaf Clear

Her eyes held me
strong as the grip
of roots to the tree.
Roots
that store
the memory of sky
through winter
when the wind
blows every leaf clear.

I fell leaf
by leaf
into the last of me.
Skin strewn –
shed to bone.
But her eyes held me,
strong as trees
bound in earth.

And in the dark
soiled winter,
my soul turned.
And like sap
to sky
rose in my veins
towards spring.

We Thought Ourselves Friends

We thought ourselves friends.
All that year
we trudged through the rain
and snow;
the slush of forest paths
in winter.
Our eyes rooted to the ground
watching each step.

Our thoughts on the past.
We talked of love and the losing of it.
Exchanged cures.
Analysed heart break;
romance and obsession.
Studying means
to survive their lure.

Then, in the way of it;
without warning,
spring came –
snow thawed,
the paths grew dry.
Above our heads
leaves sprang green.

We looked up
for the first time,
towards sky
and found we were
looking
into each other's eyes.
Once more,
hearts in peril.

Since that day,
there has been
no where else to look.

Taking Shelter

We were walking by the lake,
engaged in formal conversation
when the rain began.

We stopped for a moment under a tree.
Not much shelter but enough.
Looking out across water
towards the darkening hills;
without pausing in your talk
you caught up your hair
and with quick hands
began to wind it about your head.
(To keep it dry,
you told me later –
much later)

At the time it took me by surprise.
I watched the black strands lift clear.
The movement of your fingers –
saw your neck exposed white and bare,
the innocent provocation
of your ear.
I didn't kiss you then,
though you turned
and looked at me as if you thought I might.

But that was the moment
when you stopped and put up your hair;
holding the clips between your teeth so that
your lips drew back,
that I saw a word unspoken,
take shape between our eyes
and hover there.

Shall we go, you said,
I think it's over,
and we began to walk away
as if it were.
But like the midges
that circled at our heads,
the moment
followed after us
through the moist autumn air.

The Gaelic Poets Warned Me

The gaelic poets warned me.
They knew you of old –
your eyes like green stones
on a river bed,
the milk white skin,
the hair raven black
and its sheen.
For centuries they sang
your praise,

but I paid no attention
or had forgotten.
Until I saw you walking naked.
By then it was too late –
my past had caught up with me.
Snared by atavistic beauty,
I fell into history.
All the poems in the English language
will not save me.

When My Arm Went Round Your Waist

Where does love begin?
Where can we find
its source?
Does it start in the body
or first in the soul?
Is passion, some
fine tuned symmetry of spirit
or no more than a random
chemical reaction?

Was my love for you
ignited
by a quality of mind I saw –
through months of winter discourse
on lofty, abstract themes:
a way of seeing
the angle of your vision –
the exact slant of its light.
The courage of your dreams.

Or was it simply a fluke of the senses:
a chance encounter of memory and touch?
Whichever I select
as motive
I can define the hour
of revelation
and its place.

A summer evening;
lilac at an open door.
Someone played a slow air,
a dance was called.
I didn't know
how you would move
towards me,
or that your body
leaning into mine
would feel
taut as a sapling
and more pliant.

I didn't know how my heart would beat
or the seismic shift
it would make
in the scheme of things.
But I know
I fell in love with you
when my arm
went round your waist.

Dressing for the World

And afterwards,
I watched you
for the first time
getting ready for the world.
Lying in the warmth of our sheets,
I watched you putting on
your clothes;

carefully restoring order,
becoming once again
the woman I had known.
I watched you put on blouse
and stockings and skirt
I watched you brush your hair
the way my sister does –

all of it in one motion
swept forward
and then with a toss of the head,
all as quickly back.
I watched you put on mascara
and finally
in a last amused attempt
at camouflage – lipstick.

Does it make me look,
you asked –
like a woman who hasn't spent
the afternoon in bed?
But nothing could make you seem
again

like the woman you looked to me –
not make-up, not stockings,
not skirt:
the only woman I had known till then,
dressed and perfumed;
careful for the world.

The woman you were
three hours ago,
before you took off your clothes
in the afternoon,
and came to bed –
with a woman
without clothes.

Silk

She is over me now
dense as snow
newly laid.
White as milk.
Soft as a sheet of silk,
she covers me.
Have you ever felt
silk and satin together?
That's our skin
touching.
She is over me now
white as sea foam.
Soft as milk thistle.
She covers me
dense as snow
newly laid.
Soft as silk and satin
touching.

The Whiteness of Snow

The whiteness
of snow
on a branch of pine,
is the whiteness
of her skin
from shoulder
to thigh.
And the sway of the branch
under its
flesh of snow,
is the song of her hips
in the weight of my hands.

I saw a Fish this Morning

I saw a fish
this morning
and it looked
like you.

Leaping
clear into space;
back arched
for joy.

And I wanted to be
lake water,
cool blue, slipping from its sides.
Green reeds washing soft

around its thighs.
I wanted to be yellow river bed
sand,
hollowed for its belly.

I wanted to be bright, quick air,
waiting,
sucked by its breath.
I wanted to be

high
as spring summer sky –
sun gleaming
in its eye.

To Walk in the Street is Like Dancing

To see you walking towards me
with the swing in your hips,
the gleam in your eye.

You make me think of silver.
You shimmer and shimmy
like silver.

The sheen of your dark hair,
the gleam of your eyes,
the sway of your hips,

that long quick stride.
To see you walking towards me,
to walk in the street with you,

my arm about your waist,
your flank pressed near to mine
your white smooth side,

bound in perfect step.
To walk in the street
is like dancing.

To see the smile widen
on your wide full lips.
There is nothing as fine

as the whiteness of your smile,
widening your wide full lips.
The sheen of your hair,

the gleam of your eyes.
To walk in the street is like dancing.
The sway of your hips,

that long quick stride.
The shimmy and shimmer,
the cool heat of your eyes.

You make me think of silver;
subtle and quick,
slipping through my fingers.

At Every Window a Different Season

I remember a house
where we sat to watch
the days pass;
hour by hour.
The changing of the light
on mountain and lake.
The year's passage
in an afternoon.
At every window
a different season.

Bog and high grass
climbed the mountains
where sheep lay strewn
like white rocks,
cloud catching in their horns.
There were geese in the boreen,
cows in the hedgerows.
A church spire
and the ocean
at the foot of the garden.

On clear nights
stars shimmered
like cut glass
in the immensity of sky
that wrapped itself
and silence
from end to end of the sleeping fields.

In winter
the roar of wind
drowned speech.
Walls shook and timber.
Wave upon wave
rocked our bed,
a curragh at anchor
on the open sea.

I remember
a half door
thrown wide upon waking.
Hay stacks on the front lawn.
In summer
wild flowers rampant;
iris, primrose, foxglove.
And in the pools of sunshine after rain,
a table and chairs
of wrought iron
set out for late breakfast.

A garden adrift
between mist
and heat haze.
Palm trees,
fuchsia,
mallow.
And the wandering pathways
that led to the sea,
paved with orange flags
we carried stone by stone
from the most westerly strand
in the western world.

A house
full of cats and cooking.
Hanging baskets from the rafters;
plants in the baskets
and cats on the rafters
or sun bathing
under wide shaded pottery lamps.
A sailor's hammock,
a hearth and crane,
armchairs drawn to the fire.
Coffee on the stove,
wine on the table.
Music at three o'clock in the morning.

I remember a house
where we sat
to watch the days pass
hour by hour.
The changing of the light
over mountain and lake.
The passage of a year
in an afternoon.
At every window
a different season.

My Grandmother's Voice

Sometimes
when my mother speaks to me
I hear her mother's voice:
my grandmother's
with its trace of Belfast accent
which carried with it
something from every town
the Normans passed through.
My grandmother,
mother of seven,
who will not be quiet yet
twenty years after her death.

Sometimes when I look at my mother
it is her mother I see –
the far sighted gaze,
the way of sitting
bolt upright in a chair –
holding forth, the quick wit,
the fold her hands take in her lap.
The sweep of her hair.

And listening closely
or caught unaware,
I hear my great grandmother
echo between them:
A glance – a tone.
My grandmother's
mother

who died giving birth
to her only child.
Whose words and stories
pent up in her daughter
flowed on
into the talk of my mother.
I catch them now in my own.
My head sings with their conversation.

And hearing them –
this fertile
and ghostly orchestration –
I am sorry to have brought them
to the end of their line.
Stopped them in their track
across millenia.
From what primeval starting point
to here?
A relay race
through centuries
from mother to daughter –
an expression passed on
a gesture,
a profile.

Their voices reverberate in my head.
They will die with me.
I have put an end to inheritance –
drawn a stroke across the page.
Their grace,
their humour,
their way of walking in a room.

The stoicism
that carried them all this way
has stopped with me;
the first of their kind
who will not bear their gift
and burden.

I lift my pen
quickly, wanting
to set down all the stories
spoken by these busy, garrulous,
long lived women
who never had a moment
to sit down
or lift a pen.

I begin.
A young woman, a protestant
from Belfast,
married a sea captain,
a catholic
who drowned at sea . . .

About the Author

Mary Dorcey, born in County Dublin, Ireland, is a short story writer and poet. In 1990 she won the Rooney Prize for Irish Literature for her book *A Noise from the Woodshed* and was awarded an Art's Council bursary for literature in 1990 and 1995.

Her work is taught on Irish Studies and Women's Studies courses at universities in Ireland, Britain, Canada and America. Her poetry has been performed on stage, radio and television (RTE and Channel 4). It has also been dramatised in stage productions in Ireland and Britain – 'Sunnyside Plucked' and 'In the Pink', which toured Europe and Australia. In spring of 1995 she worked as International Writer in residence in Manchester.

Her work expresses Irish, feminist and lesbian concerns in a way that highlights the universality of human experience. She has been widely anthologised and translated into Italian, Spanish, Dutch and Japanese.

She is currently working on a new collection of short stories. Mary Dorcey lives in County Wicklow.